THE FOUR PROMISES

A journey of healing past and present trauma

DR. RONALD BELL II

SPACE FOR ME
LLC

Space for Me, LLC
St. Paul, MN 55116

Publisher: Space for Me, LLC
Project Manager: Sedrik Newbern, Newbern Consulting, LLC
Editor: Linda Wolf, Network Publishing Partners, Inc.
Cover Designer: Joshua Swodeck, Swodeck, Inc.

Printed in the United States of America
First Edition: May 2021

Scripture references, unless otherwise noted, are from the New King James Version.

ISBN Paperback: 978-0-578-90059-9

Library of Congress Control Number: 2021907934

Dedication

This book is dedicated to the community of the grieving.
May you be reminded that there is space for you.

Table of Contents

Introduction

Why This Work Matters

When did you realize what race you are? I can remember the exact day that each of my sons discovered they were Black. My oldest is 9 years old now. When he was in first grade, he came home one afternoon, extremely agitated. After an uncomfortable encounter with a classmate, he wanted to know why his skin was so different from his classmate's.

I took him outside to sit on the porch where he explained that his classmate had called him *Black* but, as he boldly and accurately pointed out, he was not black; his skin was brown. He could not understand why he was being labeled Black when his skin was brown and why his skin was so different in color than that classmate's skin was.

My son and I sat for some time on that porch. I reminded him of his grandfather and told him stories of his great-grandfather and great-great-grandfather. I showed him pictures of our family. I showed him my hand. I explained to him, "Son, we share the same skin. It is your mother's skin, your grandfather's, your great-great-grandfather's; it is your cousins' and aunts' and uncles' skin. This is our family skin. It connects us. It marks us. We wear this skin with pride."

I watched his sad, confused countenance begin to shift and brighten. He sat up straight and smiled as he started naming his cousins and making the connection between their skin and his. That day I watched my son embrace the fact that he was Black. His journey to Blackness was in stark contrast to my younger son's.

My younger son was 5 when he discovered he was Black. George Floyd had been murdered by Minneapolis police the day before his discovery. We were living in Saint Paul at that time, where I was pastoring a church in the area. I was preparing to distribute food for those in need who had been affected by the previous night's riots. The energy was tense.

People were in pain; our hearts were broken for how we had been treated. The news was flooded with images of protests and riots, replays of the murder of Floyd, and commentary on injustice for African Americans. That day we had coordinated with the Pan Hellenic council and Black Greek fraternities and sororities in the area to hold a successful food giveaway. We expected to feed between 500 and 1,000 people that day. There would be hundreds of people coming to drop off food and hundreds of other people coming to receive food. I knew I could not shelter my 5-year-old from the reality which was about to bombard him.

My wife and I sat him and his brother down that morning and had the talk. We told them about George Floyd; we explained to him what the police officer did and why it was wrong. We tried as best we could to pivot the discussion to our response as community members, in serving and supporting each other. Instead my 5-year-old son kept asking over and over again, "What did Floyd do?"

I could tell his brain was trying to make sense of what happened. He was slowly, mentally deconstructing all of those societal constructs he had come to believe in – namely "Police are good and here to help you," and "Bad guys are bad and the police are there to stop them." None of those constructs made sense anymore to him.

I watched his face contort and change as he realized that the only crime George Floyd committed was looking like us, sharing the same skin that we have. That skin like his father and mother, that skin like his cousins and aunts and uncles, grandparents and great-grandparents... that skin like his. That day I watched my younger son discover that he was Black. His journey had begun.

Each of us is well acquainted with loss. I do not simply mean the loss of loved ones, though that grief captures each of us.

Instead, I am talking about the loss of humanization. What makes us human is our capacity to live in connection with one another. That capacity is constantly being strained and altered, given new historical content, self-awareness, and revelations. We are in a perpetual process of remaking and redefining our humanness in relation to other humans.

I watched my two sons struggle with this concept as they discovered their Blackness. However, in fairness, it is a struggle that we all wrestle with, mainly because everyone we encounter is involved in their own process of redefining and remaking, also in relation to us. As a result of this parallel work, each of us carries trauma that is both interrelated and individual – a racialized trauma. Racial trauma is not exclusive to African Americans. In fact, it is sewn into the fabric of this nation, it is a part of our history as a nation as well as our present, and if we do nothing more, it will be a part of our future.

Resmaa Menakem, in his groundbreaking work *My Grandmother's Hands*, wrote, "Unhealed trauma acts like a rock a thrown into a pond; it causes ripples that move outward, affecting many other bodies over time." Over time that unhealed trauma presents as culture; it becomes baked into the character of our relations with each other, Black and white. Over time, that unhealed, racialized trauma creates invisible social borders that effectively reinforce the mythologies that this trauma promulgated. It should be clear that when unhealed trauma metastasizes as culture and gets passed down through generations, it becomes increasingly impossible to empathize with a group or individual existing outside one's racialized traumatic frame.

You cannot empathize with something or someone you do not recognize as equal in value to yourself. The more we subconsciously reinforce the mythologies of this trauma, the more we further isolate and distance ourselves from each other, until we become unrecognizable as human to each other. This is the ultimate danger of racialized trauma and thus the ultimate danger of trauma in and of itself – its ability to distort and dehumanize. Therefore, each of us must embrace our own trauma and begin to do the work of healing.

I thought I had begun to do that work. However, the morning after the murder of George Floyd, a Black man unjustifiably killed as a direct action of Minneapolis police, I received a call from the mayor's office. The protest and subsequent riots that had blanketed the night and spilled into that morning were beginning to reveal a deeper plot at hand. The mayor's office informed me that they had obtained information that organizations affiliated with white nationalists had infiltrated the previous night's protest and spearheaded the rioting we witnessed. These groups had left documents revealing that their intended goal was to destroy Black businesses that operated in predominantly Black neighborhoods, as well as influential Black churches, like the one I pastored. The mayor's office had one request: Board up your windows and doors as quickly as you can and get home safely.

That morning as I pulled into the church parking lot, I expected to see shattered glass lining our entrance, broken windows, burned-out rooms, or graffitied walls. Instead, I found a quiet, almost serene environment. In truth, the air smelled of a mixture of tear-gas, burnt wood, and smoldering rubber. There were National Guard helicopters hovering overhead, armored tanks along with trucks full of police driving up and down the streets, and the sounds of fire engines and police sirens filling the air. But at the church, all was quiet.

Dr. Tanden Brekke, a faculty member at Bethel University and a tenant of one of our office spaces at the church, happened to be at the church when I arrived. I came ready to clean and board up the church. Seeing no need, Dr. Brekke and I decided to grab brooms, trash bags, and gloves and check on our neighbors in the community who were not as fortunate as we were.

I want you to picture this image: two men, two fathers, two husbands, two Christians, two doctoral graduates cleaning up the community. Now dilute that perspective to just one qualifier: a Black man and a white man traumatized by the previous night's events, now seeking solace by re-engaging the community in a practice of healing.

We were both grieving. Both of us were victims to the trauma we had witnessed in our neighborhood just a day earlier with the killing of George Floyd. Both of us were wrestling with trying to make meaning and find language to describe our individual trauma experience and its tentacles that were still rigidly attached to the historical racialized trauma living in each of our bones.

I knew that we had to deal with the trauma. We, as a community, needed to sit in the discomfort and anxiety to wait, listen, and be present. We could not simply rush to previous failed attempts at reconciliation. We needed to be present. We needed to find a way – not to circumvent, but to exist in trauma – to heal. At the church, we set up a community trauma healing day, to which we invited counselors, therapists, and psychologists to offer free services to the community. We put together over 100 trauma healing bags for kids in the community, and we began plans for outfitting the church with its own trauma healing center. All these shifts were guided by one core belief: This trauma isn't going away, and we have to address it.

Some time ago I led a discussion with a group of social workers who asked me to speak about tools for helping their clients of color find appropriate resources for reconciling the racial trauma they were experiencing. Most of the social workers and therapists on the webinar were white women, and most of the clients they were referencing were Black men. What I discovered was they were attempting to solve the trauma of Blackness. They were attempting to find one solution, one cure that would somehow magically heal their Black clients from having to endure racialized trauma. They were trying to fix race. Racialized trauma, like most trauma, is complex. It is ongoing, deep-seated, and present.

Instead of trying to fix the trauma, I outlined tools for helping clients continue a healthy, manageable existence in trauma. The four promises you will read in this book are some of those tools. They are designed to reallocate authority of our personhood to ourselves, instead of allowing the trauma we experience to rule our existence. These promises are effective for anyone dealing with ongoing, continuous trauma. They are appropriate for anyone encountering complex present trauma, whether that trauma is related to race, environment, economic factors, culture, or sex. These promises help us endure and survive.

Origin Story of the Four Promises

"It's not the load that breaks you down;
it's the way you carry it."
Lena Horne

My Aunt Emma was an evangelist in the Church of God in Christ (COGIC). She was a beautiful and powerful woman. She could command a room with just a glance, a smile, or a breath. She was the kind of woman in whose presence you dared not show up if you had been doing anything she might deem as unholy or ungodly, because she was going to call it out and tell you about yourself. The summer I began undergraduate studies, I was privileged to spend each weekend with her. I played saxophone for the church's band and attended every service. That was my first experience of COGIC worship, and it was otherworldly.

People would come early for what they called "testimony service." During this time, people could share with the church members any problems or challenges in their lives and receive encouragement. I would listen to what seemed like the most dreadful stories, but I noticed something: As people told their horrific, sad stories, they did so with a degree of excitement, pointing to God's activity and intervention and not to the challenge or trauma itself. As they told their stories, they often would begin to shout and dance, and soon the musicians would be signaled by the organist to begin playing. For several minutes, through playing, dancing, and singing we would refashion the traumatic stories of the narrator into a story of victory and opportunity for celebration. Those who told their stories would leave renewed and ready to go back into their ongoing trauma with a new level of determination.

What was going on here? The people were giving themselves permission to be fully present in their trauma. They were not shrinking from it or covering it up but instead were exposing and displaying it for all to see. This was critical because you can't heal what you keep hiding. But they were not just giving themselves permission; they were also engaging in a ritual that included playing, dancing, and singing. They were not allowing the trauma to cause them to be stuck. They were using their bodies, freeing themselves of the stress, weight, and burden of the trauma they carried.

They were also doing this in a sacred place. They had found a circle, a community of like-minded people, where they could heal and be valued. This is important because you cannot heal in solitude. Lastly, they were controlling their narrative. They were retelling their traumatic stories during testimony service from a new lens, a new perspective that shifted the power dynamic away from the trauma and back into their grasp.

These four methods of managing ongoing, complex trauma through the power of testimony service that I witnessed that summer in the COGIC church helped frame for us the four promises we each must choose if we are to manage our own complex present trauma experiences. Here they are in order:

1. I promise to give myself permission to be fully present in my trauma.
2. I promise to find and/or create rituals that allow me to begin to heal while still in my trauma experience.
3. I promise to find and/or create circles where I can heal while still in my trauma experience.
4. I promise to take authority over the telling of my trauma story from a position that promotes my health.

In the sections to come, we will go in depth with each of these promises, showing how, when properly applied, they can positively affect the complex trauma being experienced. It is my hope that you will engage with the material, the tools, the questions, and the devotional. This work is designed to help you manage and live a healthy existence while still experiencing ongoing trauma. Regardless of the source of the trauma – race, environment, economics, sex, finances, politics, and so on – these promises work.

Section I: Centering Opportunities

"The impatient idealist says: 'Give me a place to stand and I shall move the earth.' But such a place does not exist. We all have to stand on the earth itself and go with her at her pace."

Chinua Achebe

Before we begin to study the four promises, there are three opportunities I want to invite us to take to center ourselves and be present.

Centering Opportunity 1: The Gratefulness Exercise

What are five things that are challenging or pushing on you emotionally right now?

(Example: I have two young children who have been out of school for over a year because of the COVID-19 pandemic and its impact on schools. I've watched my sons change; they are more isolated now. Their level of engagement and wonder is different than it was last year. I worry for them.)

What are your five?

1. _____

   _____

2. _____

   _____

3. _____

_____

4. _____

_____

5 _____

_____

After you have listed your five challenges, now write down five things you are grateful about for those same challenges.

(Example: Even though my children have been home for over a year, I am so grateful I have had the opportunity to spend so much time with them. I can see them maturing. It's been a complete joy watching their personalities develop and getting the chance to help shape and encourage them.)

What are your five?

1. _____

_____

2. _____

_____

3. _____

4. _____

5. _____

Why is this exercise important? It helps shift our perspective and allow our brains to operate from a settled, peaceful mode instead of a traumatic, anxious one. When we engage new information from a traumatic, anxious, stress-filled posture, we distill the information differently than we would if we engaged from a steady, serene one. From a traumatic, anxious posture, our brains are looking for negativity; they are wired to look for threats, and so we close ourselves off to accepting new information because it may be a danger.

From a traumatic, anxious posture, we begin to give short, monosyllabic, curt responses. We do this unconsciously because our brains are in survival mode. This exercise helps us come out of that trauma mode and begin to process from a higher level. This exercise helps us open up and be fully present.

Centering Opportunity 2: Check-In Exercise

In the book, *The Triune Brain in Evolution* (1990), neuroscientist Paul D. MacLean describes three distinct sections of the brain. The first is the primitive brain or reptilian complex. This portion of the brain is responsible for our fight-flight-freeze responses. It regulates our survival functions. The second is our limbic system or paleomammalian complex. It is responsible for our emotions. Our limbic system helps us regulate how we feel and react to the world. Last is our neocortex or neomammalian complex. This portion of our brain is responsible for critical thinking. It processes and sorts information. These three sections are critical to proper brain function and serve important and distinct roles. Each one tells us something about how we are engaging and interpreting the world.

In this exercise, I want us to check in by answering these three questions:

1. What is your body telling you right now about how you are situated and engaged in the world around you?

(Example: My shoulders feel tense and heavy, my hands are clenched, and my heart is beating fast.)

_____

_____

2. How do you feel right now in this moment?

(Example: I feel nervous and unsettled, as if there is some impending doom crouching just off in the distance.)

_____

_____

3. How would you describe the state of your mind right now? Is it like a peaceful, quiet lake, or like a powerful, unrelenting waterfall?

(Example answer: It's hard for me to focus right now. I've got so much going on in my head that I feel mentally cluttered.)

_____

_____

The answers to this check-in exercise help us orient ourselves. These answers give us permission to be fully aware of how we are engaging the world around us. They help us determine whether we are in the best position to receive new information or if we need to take some time to regulate our emotional state.

In my experience, when working with married or engaged couples, I often observe a disconnect between their body posture and tone of voice versus their words. Their body posture looks tense, their tone sounds defensive, and yet with their words they proclaim that they are "fine" or "okay." This indicates that they are unable to receive new information openly. Their brains are in survival and defense mode. This exercise helps them acknowledge that truth and take the time necessary to recalibrate so that they can move forward.

Centering Opportunity 3: Logging in-Exercise

In *The Body Keeps the Score*, author Dr. Bessel van der Kolk shares that "Dissociation is the essence of trauma." When we experience a traumatic event or are engaged in an ongoing traumatic experience, our brains, as a method of survival, will often split off and fragment the experience's "emotions, sounds, images, thoughts, [and] physical sensations related to the trauma" as a way to protect us during that survival mode. This means our brains have crafted a way for us to emotionally check out. If we are not careful, we can remain in that "checked-out" mode long after the traumatic experience has passed. This exercise helps us reconnect to our bodies and to our present experiences.

Five Questions: Every time you revisit this exercise, change up the order of the questions (as well as the number of examples to provide for each sense) to further challenge yourself.

5. What are five things in your environment right now that you can touch?

(Example: cell phone, coffee cup, pen, drapes, picture frame)

_____

_____

4. What are four things in your environment right now that you can smell?

(Example: coffee, the heat from the air vent, a scented candle, hand soap on my hands)

_____

_____

3. What are three things in your environment right now that you can hear?

(Example: the clothes dryer buzzing, my son's computer game, the creak of the office chair)

_____

_____

2. What are two things in your environment right now that you can taste?

(Example: coffee, aftertaste of breakfast)

_____

_____

1. What is one thing in your environment right now that you can see?

(Example: books on the shelf)

_____

_____

This exercise helps you log in and be present. It reminds you that you can be fully present in this lived experience. Changing the order and number of examples for each of the five senses each time you use this exercise will help deepen your awareness of the present moment. This, in turn, helps to diminish the power of past and present trauma by learning to center your attention on what is really happening right now instead.

Section II: The Four Promises

Promise #1

I promise to give myself permission to be fully present in my trauma.

"I shall become, I shall become a collector of me.
And put meat on my soul."
Sonia Sanchez

Permission

In *Concept of Emotion Viewed from a Prototype Perspective*, Fehr and Russell wrote, "Everyone knows what an emotion is, until asked to give a definition. Then, it seems, no one knows." In truth, there are hundreds of emotions, ranging from happiness to apathy, fear to desire, and so on. Each of those emotional responses are informative. They are helpful both to us and to others. They can be a warning, an invitation for mating, a clue to potential poison, or even a signal to rest. Embracing our emotions is critical. It is one of the ways our bodies speak to and direct us.

At our core, we have six basic emotions that all others build upon: anger, fear, happiness, sadness, disgust, and surprise, according to Paul Ekman. Alessia Celeghin and a team of psychologists stated, "From a psychological perspective, an emotion is basic only if it does not contain another emotion, that is, if it represents an atomic, irreducible psychological construct." These six emotions are universal, meaning that, as humans, each of us possesses them, regardless of race, gender, socioeconomic status, background, or geographic location. Knowing that these emotions are universal can help us engage the world. They are a necessary part of our socioemotional maturity and our ability to lead and communicate with others.

Yet somehow life has also taught us to hide our core emotions. Life has instructed us not to openly express anger, fear, happiness, sadness, disgust, or surprise. Life has instructed us to suppress our core emotions and replace them with responses we deem as acceptable to others, though inauthentic to ourselves. So, we may feal fear, but in the company of others we express courage. We may feel happy, but in the company of others we express apathy. We may feel sadness, but in the company of others we express indifference. These complicated responses serve no one. In fact, they signal to others that something inauthentic is occurring. Feeling one way and communicating another is not beneficial to either party.

As leaders, we are quick to display these complications, hiding our core emotions for the sake of appeasing an assumed norm. The problem, however, is magnified when it involves leaders because not only does the continuation of this act present a personal emotional injury, but, because leaders serve as models, it also signals to others that this is the behavior to emulate. It signals to others that they, too, should hide their true emotional responses. Leaders perpetuate the cycle by not being true to themselves.

Why do we do this? Why do we both present complicated emotional responses and also prohibit ourselves from being authentic with our own emotions? One word: Shame. Brené Brown gives an excellent definition of shame in relation to guilt, suggesting, "Shame is 'I am bad.' Guilt is 'I did something bad.'"

Shame is an internal response to external factors. Shame is a decision on identity. Shame is our inner self defining our outer self. Shame is entirely self-directed, self-engineered, and self-sustained. Others could, by their actions, assign guilt to us about a particular circumstance, but shame is something we choose all on our own.

Shame is a tertiary combination of disgust and fear. It is the combination of two major core emotions – fear, which alerts us to potential danger, and disgust, which alerts us to potential poisons or uncomfortable situations. Shame is a powerful emotion. Shame has also been described as maladaptive because it encourages dysfunctional behaviors, particularly behavioral avoidance, according to June P. Tangney and others. It is my contention that shame is at the center of our desire to present complicated emotional responses. More so, it is the foundation for our tendency to be inauthentic with ourselves about our own emotions.

Take this hypothetical situation as an example. What would happen if a leader of an army ran onto the battlefield and announced to his fellow soldiers that he was afraid? Fear is a core emotion and would be a completely natural and understandable response to their current circumstance. The leader's concern for not sharing that emotion would have nothing to do with his own assessment of their abilities to do the job; the leader's concern would be that the presence and expression of that particular emotion would paint him as being weak or unfit to lead in the minds of his troops. So, the leader shutters that emotion and instead stands before the soldiers to project courage.

The leader is truly afraid. The leader's shame is connected to not being able to fully express his own basic, core emotions that would make him vulnerable to the perceptions of others and, in his mind, reclassify him as equal in power and authority to all others. So, the avoidant behavior that typically accompanies shame is used to alter the leader's emotional responses, and over time the leader becomes inauthentic to his own emotions.

The unique paradox is that, had the leader simply been honest with his soldiers, he would have discovered an emotional freedom that would have allowed him to connect and lead on a deeper level. Remember, those core emotions are universal. Chances are if you are feeling fear, so is the person you are talking to; if you are feeling sad or happy or disgusted, so is the person occupying the same circumstance you are in. The myth is that uncovering and expressing our core emotions makes us weak. The reality is that the ability of a leader to express his core emotions is an asset. It promotes confidence in others who were sensing something but were unable or unwilling to lean into it. Again, when we express our core emotions, it gives us an emotional freedom.

Do you remember that song from your childhood, "If You're Happy and You Know It?" The fundamental theory behind that song was to give yourself permission to express your emotions. That song is a rallying cry for authentic emotional responses. When we give ourselves permission to be fully happy, sad, afraid, disgusted, angry, or surprised, we free ourselves from emotional complications and can begin to redirect those freed-up energies toward healing, clarity, or even rest. Our bodies are wired for this.

Did you know that you have three different types of tears: basal, reflex, and emotional? Basal tears keep the eye moisturized; they coat the eye and protect it from drying out. Reflex tears flush out the eye if an irritant is present. Lastly, emotional tears are produced in response to a feeling. Each type of tears has a different chemical compound – they are fundamentally different tears.

Scientists have found that our emotional tears have stress chemicals in them; they stimulate the body to produce endorphins, which are known to be the "feel-good" chemicals produced by the brain. Our body is waiting for us to allow ourselves to embrace our emotions so that it can do the work it was designed to do. Our bodies are waiting for us to allow ourselves to be fully present in our own emotions, fully present in our own trauma, fully present in our own grief. So, the first promise we need to make with ourselves is to give ourselves permission to be fully present, to fully embrace those core emotions, and to be authentic with where and how we are.

Exercise: Permission

Look at this hub of basic emotions. What is helpful about this tool for you in describing and defining your emotional state?

_____

_____

What are some ways you could integrate this hub into interactions with your leadership teams or family structures?

_____

_____

How do you feel right now and why? Use the hub to locate your emotion.

_____

_____

Which of the six core emotions do you feel you express most often and why?

_____

_____

Which of the six core emotions is the most challenging for you to express and why?

_____

_____

When you are feeling fear, what do you think your body is telling you to do?

_____

_____

When you are feeling disgusted, what warning might your body be giving you?

_____

_____

Do you often listen to your emotions and to your body?

_____

_____

Our core emotions are universal, meaning everyone has them. Which of those core emotions is the most challenging for you to recognize in other people and why?

_____

_____

Why do you think we hide our core emotions from others?

_____

_____

Who in your life would you consider as emotionally healthy? How freely does that person express emotions?

_____

_____

Who in your life would you consider as emotionally unhealthy? How does that person express emotions?

_____

_____

What traits from those relationships have you used to build your own emotional responses?

_____

_____

How do you think feelings of shame have impacted your relationships with others?

_____

_____

Why do you think it's important to be authentic in how you express your emotions?

_____

_____

The Plan: Permission

What will you commit to today when it comes to giving yourself permission to express your true feelings?

_____

_____

What measures can you put in place to hold yourself accountable to this plan?

_____

_____

How will you celebrate, having completed this goal today?

_____

_____

Promise #2

I promise to find and/or create rituals that allow me to begin to heal while still in my trauma experience.

"Dancing is more than the locomotive movement of the body because of a rhythm. The locomotion of the body is just an outward expression of something that is genuine, deep, and resonates with your core."
Paul Bamikole

Rituals

Spanish neuroscientist Santiago Ramón y Cajal once said, "Every man can, if he so desires, become the sculptor of his own brain." In *The Body Keeps the Score,* Dr. Bessel van der Kolk says that "as long as trauma is unresolved, the stress hormones that the body secretes to protect itself keep circulating, and defensive movements and emotional responses keep getting replayed." When we don't address trauma or simply try to deny its existence, we are literally sculpting for ourselves a dysfunctional and toxic reality. It's a toxicity that is both theoretical and literal. That unresolved trauma is present in our bodies. Therefore, how we choose to think about something and what we do with those thoughts regulates how we experience the world both tangibly and intangibly.

If asked to think critically about a traumatic, life-defining event, many of us, while recalling the matter, would begin to feel the weight of that event somewhere in our bodies. Perhaps our chest would feel tight, our shoulders heavy. Perhaps our palms would begin to sweat, or our backs become uncomfortable. When I think about a really traumatic or rough season in my life, my stomach feels bloated and uneasy. This is because trauma is embodied.

Our brains are incredible machines. Our brains have one core mission: survival. When we experience trauma, our brain goes into overtime safeguarding us so that it can prevent any future trauma from occurring. Over 80 billion neurons move at lightning speeds, making new connections with each other, all for the sole purpose of protection. So, that memory and energy of the traumatic encounter gets stored in our bodies as a reminder of the experience to prepare us for any future attacks. Our brain is just doing its job by embodying trauma.

That trauma moves freely throughout the body via our autonomic nervous system, a series of nerves that connect our spine to most of our organs and limbs. When trauma or stress occurs, the nervous system goes on high alert, pushing blood out to our limbs and major organs. Our palms sweat, our pupils dilate, our hearts pump faster, and our lungs take short, quick breaths. All of this is preparation for the trauma and stress we are feeling.

It's interesting that while our autonomic nervous system is pushing blood out to our extremities to defend us, it is taking that blood from somewhere. The blood is being pulled from other vital organs. In *Brain, Attachment, Personality: An Introduction to Neuro-affective Development*, Susan Hart says that "the blood comes from the core of our body; the core that facilitates digestion, repairs the immune system, and manages the equilibrium of cellular processes and basic brain functions."

In short, when we are involved in a trauma episode, our digestion, immune system's health, and ability to process information using critical thinking through normal brain functions are severely affected. Now imagine an ongoing traumatic event or unresolved trauma. Those same core functions continue to be affected while our brain remains in a state of traumatic response.

Imagine for a moment a young impala in the forest, grazing in a beautiful, open field. While grazing, the young impala detects the scent of many large male lions. Within seconds, the impala hears the growl of those lions and feels the ground pulsating from the weight of their approach. The impala has nowhere to run. It also cannot outmatch the lions, and so something very interesting happens. The brain of the impala goes into freeze mode. Its autonomic nervous system sends signals throughout the body to pull all available blood and direct it completely to the extremities. As a result, the impala's heart rate and mental functions decrease, and lung functions suffer. In effect, the impala becomes frozen. The impala doesn't fight or flee; instead it freezes.

The impala freezes as a defensive mechanism. Its brain is hoping the approaching animals will see it as dead meat and go off to find a live challenge instead. It's hardwired to do this. The same is true in humans: We freeze. All the unresolved trauma convinces our brains and autonomic nervous system that we are in danger. So, emotionally, we freeze. We get stuck. We are unable to proceed past the unresolved trauma or ongoing situation. That same pull of blood from our core to our extremities leaves us not only emotional frozen but also susceptible to digestive and immune problems, as well as unable to make critical, healthy decisions for ourselves. Think about the times in your life when you felt emotionally stuck due to a traumatic event. You probably also had weight/digestive or memory issues or were sicker than usual. That is the brain at work.

The impala teaches us not only how to freeze but also how to unfreeze. In the article "When Trauma Gets Stuck in the Body," Beth Shaw informs us that "when animals suffer trauma… they will literally shake it off, which helps the animal discharge the energy of the traumatic event." Shaw says that "shaking or trembling, which comes from the limbic brain (the part of the brain that holds emotions), sends a signal that the danger has passed and that the fight-or-flight system can turn off. They are literally finishing the nervous system response to release the traumatic experience from the body."

This shaking or trembling is embodied healing. Just as trauma is embodied, so also is healing. What we do with our bodies signals to our brains that the traumatic event, i.e., the danger, has passed. As humans, much like the impala, we must find individual ways of shaking it off, embodying our own healing. This is the importance of creating rituals. Rituals get our body moving. They pull us out of our traumatic response and into practices that signal to our brain that we can begin to release what we are carrying. Rituals help us heal.

Circling back to the people who found release from their traumas at the COGIC church service through movement, your healing rituals could be as simple as stretching, dancing, exercising, shopping, or going for a walk to enjoy nature. Many people find healing through journaling about the experience. The rituals can also be unique to us, like eating a certain meal or putting on a particular hat. The goal is to create a ritual that helps us shake off the embodied trauma that we are carrying and begin to experience embodied healing.

Exercise: Rituals

What has been your traditional way of responding to trauma, and has it been beneficial?

_____

_____

Have you noticed places where you need to work more intensively on your reactions and responses to trauma? What are they?

_____

_____

When you feel trauma or stress, does it manifest in a certain part of your body? If so, where?

_____

_____

Do you recognize the existence of trauma in your body easily, or does it take you a while to realize you have been affected by an experience?

_____

_____

What does it mean to you that the refusal to deal with trauma and stress leaves you susceptible to diseases and sickness?

_____

_____

Can you describe a time in your life when you handled a trauma and began to feel physically better?

_____

_____

Describe a time in your life when you have felt stuck or like you were in freeze mode. What rituals helped you during those moments of freeze? In what ways did you move your body and shake it off?

_____

_____

Can you notice that freeze mode in others?

_____

_____

As you think about your current traumatic experiences, what rituals can you put in place so that you can shake the trauma off?

_____

_____

The Plan: Rituals

What will you commit to today when it comes to creating rituals that will help you embrace the trauma you are experiencing?

_____

_____

What measures can you put in place to hold yourself accountable to this plan?

_____

_____

How will you celebrate, having completed this goal today?

_____

_____

Promise #3

I promise to find and/or create circles where I can heal while still in my trauma experience.

"Age is getting to know all the ways the world turns, so that if you cannot turn the world the way you want, you can at least get out of the way so you won't get run over."
Miriam Makeba

Circles

Circles are critical. In an article entitled "An Ecological View of Psychological Trauma and Trauma Recovery," Mary Harvey says that "individual reactions to events are best understood in light of the values, behaviors, skills, and understandings that human communities cultivate in their members." Thus, trauma can only be fully understood and expressed through community. Only in community are we able to give definition to our experiences as we align them to the norms around us. For example, if we grew up in toxic spaces where everyone around us was hostile, defensive, combative, and dismissive, we may not realize that we were being traumatized because that toxicity was normalized in our community and in our circles.

Not knowing of the existence of trauma, however, does not preclude the effects of trauma from taking a toll on our bodies, perspectives, and choices. Our brains are still wired for survival, and so we remain in that freeze mode. This means our health, digestive system, heart, and lungs suffer. Our ability to think critically and make informed, quality decisions suffers. All of this is because our brains, in survival mode, are pulling blood away from our vital organs to our extremities for defense mode. Now imagine an entire community like this.

Now imagine that level of toxicity, reinforced generation after generation in communities and circles where trauma continued to go unaddressed. Therefore, we have to be critical of circles. Circles are relationships of vulnerability. They are spaces in which each of us finds community, where we can experience a sense of belonging. If we are not careful, those spaces can be toxic. They can subconsciously reinforce and normalize the trauma that we have experienced. Those circles that pacify trauma are unhelpful. We need circles of light and healing.

Hector Chiboola, in his article entitled "Theoretical Perspective of Traditional Counseling," says that the "traditional [Western] counseling process centers on four aspects: traditional counselor, client, family, and community. The key elements that inform the theoretical framework of traditional counseling from an African perspective are: cultural context, collective belief system, and initiation rituals." What Chiboola explains is that for many Western cultures, when someone is dealing with trauma, the response is to go see another individual for help. Whatever support is needed is provided through counseling in one-on-one relationships, and then, when appropriate, is shared with the person's family before being put into full practice in a community. For Western thought, community (or circles) are the last resort for engaging trauma and dealing with healing.

In traditional African perspectives on trauma, the community is engaged early when a person has encountered trauma. In many tribes, for example, when someone encounters trauma, he or she is brought to the elders of the community. The person is embraced by the community and reminded of the collective belief system. As a part of the healing journey, instead of spending time in one-on-one counseling sessions as would occur in Western perspectives, Africans invite the one traumatized to participate in a new initiation and new rituals. These practices help reconnect the person to community immediately. They help the person find healing in relationship to community. Healing happens in circles.

When we look at practices of engaging trauma, whether the Western approach that ends with the individual re-engaging the community or the African approach that starts with the individual re-engaging the community, it is clear that the community or the circle we align ourselves with is a critical part of our healing.

There are many different types of circles. The most obvious is our family; however, this may be the most toxic. In addition to family, there are affinity circles. For example, I am an avid Jeep Wrangler fan. I own a Jeep; in fact, as I write this, I am on my fifth Jeep. I love to peruse Jeep websites, attend Jeep excursion days, and read online Jeep forums. The Jeep community is a circle for me. It is a space where I can retreat when the world seems overwhelming or when the present trauma becomes too much for me to handle. I can go online, enter a forum, and connect with a group of people to simply bond over our love for Jeeps. The people who attend the gym at the same time as you do can be a circle; your friends can be a circle; your spouse can be a circle; even nature can be a circle. A circle is any space in which you find a sense of belonging and where you can be vulnerable.

The key is to find circles of light and healing, spaces that are not toxic from unresolved trauma. You cannot heal in toxicity. Imagine that I cut my hand and had an open wound. If I took my hand with the open wound and stuck it in mud, would the hand heal? The answer is no. In order to heal, in order to manage the current trauma we experience daily, we have to do the hard work of not retreating but instead allowing ourselves to be present in healthy, life-giving spaces – healthy, life-giving circles.

Exercise: Circles

How many circles can you name that you are connected to right now? Describe them.

_____

_____

In how many of those circles are you challenged, stretched, and held accountable? Describe the makeup of those circles.

_____

_____

In how many of your circles are you the leader? What does that feel like?

_____

_____

If you could create the perfect circle for yourself right now, what would be some of the key elements?

_____

_____

What are some red flags or areas of concern that you are aware of when it comes to your current circles?

_____

_____

What will it take for you step out and find new circles?

_____

_____

Can you see how challenging it is to think critically when you are connected to toxic circles? Discuss any of those experiences you have had before?

_____

_____

How did you separate yourself from those toxic circles? What was the principal motivator that allowed you to break free?

_____

_____

The Plan: Circles

What will you commit to today when it comes to creating and locating circles that will help you embrace the trauma you are experiencing?

_____

_____

What measures can you put in place to hold yourself accountable to this plan?

_____

_____

How will you celebrate, having completed this goal today?

_____

_____

Promise #4

I promise to take authority over the telling of my trauma story from a position that promotes my health.

"You have to decide who you are and force the world to deal with you, not with its idea of you."
James Baldwin

Stories

My first year as an undergraduate was one of the most fun years of my life. I had received a scholarship to play saxophone at Morgan State University in Baltimore, Maryland, and I loved it. I was part of the marching band, jazz band, and concert band. I was also active in my church band and had my own band on the side. We played for jazz clubs in Baltimore and for two different churches on Sundays. I was doing a lot of music that year and making really good money. On Mother's Day, I was at the car wash on Edmondson Avenue in Baltimore with my brand-new, all-Black, Honda Accord with brown leather interior, moon roof, and chrome rims. I had just come from playing at a church, had money in my pocket, and was grateful for life. While I was at the car wash, a man pulled out a sawed-off shotgun, pressed it into my side, cocked the gun back, and told me to give him everything I had.

I felt my spirit leave my body. I had frozen, but my heart was racing. I could feel the heat of the gun in my side as if he had already pulled the trigger. Just then, I heard a voice that I am certain was God: "Son, get out of the car." It was as if time went off pause and began to speed up. I exited the car, and the man drove off with my brand-new Honda and my saxophone in the backseat.

There are a few ways to tell that story. One way of telling that story is from the perspective of a victim. It is an honest and accurate account of the story. I was robbed at gunpoint. I had every ounce of certainty that I was going to lose my life. I could have died. All those factors are true and constitute a complete account of the events of that day.

Another way of telling that story is this: My father was a preacher, and at the time of his death, he had pastored for over 40 years. I grew up in the church, and I was a musician. I grew up traveling and playing for churches. I never had a real personal relationship with God. I never had an intention to be a preacher, and honestly, I always questioned people when they said stuff like "God says" or "The Lord told me." In fact, though my father was a pastor and I did play for multiple churches, I wasn't a member of any church. Nor did

I attend any Bible studies, pray regularly, or even pay tithe. It wasn't until the day I was robbed at gunpoint, on Mother's Day on Edmondson Avenue in Baltimore, that I heard God for myself for the first time ever. I felt God speak to me that day, and God said to me, "Son, get out of the car." I heard the Lord call me "Son," and my life has never been the same since.

The story is still the same. All the same facts are still there. I was a musician, and I was carjacked at gunpoint on Mother's Day, but this telling of the story is different. The perspective of the story is not one of a victim but instead one of a survivor. This view invites me back into the story in a way that empowers me while still addressing the trauma that was present. It does not negate the trauma or make light of the instance. It does not shrink from the weight of the circumstance. Instead, when I retell the narrative from an alternate perspective, I am allowing myself to take authority over the story instead of allowing the story to be ruled by and told through the lens of trauma alone.

Oftentimes when working with clients or church members, I will use this technique. The question I will ask when they relay stories of trauma is, "Who is the narrator of this story?" and "If there was another voice that could tell this story, what would it sound like?" One the tools that's most helpful for discovering that survivalist voice is a narrative history graph.

This graph helps us look analytically at the relationships and intersectionality of our previous traumatic life experiences.

It works like this. You begin by drawing a line graph. You mark on the graph four or five instances in your past that come immediately to your mind as severely traumatic. Then you list a date for each one and go through each event, asking the same three questions:

1) What do you want to let go of from that experience?

2) What did you learn about yourself from that experience?

3) What would you say if you could go back and speak to that younger version of yourself?

This work takes time. It is best done with a partner with whom you can be vulnerable.

This exercise helps us gather emotions, insights, and tools from our own past traumatic experiences that give us a renewed sense of power and authority to take control over the narrative of the current trauma we are experiencing. We can retell our stories in a new way that gives us authority despite the very real and present trauma we are still carrying. This method is critical in managing complex past trauma or present traumatic stress.

Exercise: Stories

NARRATIVE HISTORY GRAPH

MOM'S HOUSE   COLLEGE DORM   BEST FRIEND'S   DEATH OF JAMES
                                          BACHELOR PARTY

1964 ------ 1972 ------ 1985 --- 1993

(Sample graph: You will choose your own dates and number of traumatic events to work through.)

This exercise takes time. Are you willing to give yourself the time necessary to look at your past?

_____

_____

Is there someone you feel comfortable partnering with to do this work?

_____

_____

As you look back at each experience individually, what do you want to put behind you?

_____

_____

What did you learn about yourself from that experience?

_____

_____

What would you say if you could go back in time to advise your younger self during that experience?

_____

_____

As you look back at all the previous traumatic events that you have survived, how does this exercise help you embrace your current trauma?

_____

_____

If you could rewrite your story today, what would you say about the trauma you are experiencing now from your past traumatic experiences?

_____

_____

The Plan: Stories

What will you commit to today to create a new narrative in your own words that will help you embrace the trauma you are experiencing?

_____

_____

What measures can you put in place to hold yourself accountable to this plan?

_____

_____

How will you celebrate, having completed this goal today?

_____

_____

Section III: Activating the Four Promises

"Every great dream begins with a dreamer. Always remember, you have within you the strength, the patience, and the passion to reach for the stars to change the world."
Harriet Tubman

I ran track and field in high school. The 300- and 110-meter hurdles were my favorite events to run. I was not the fastest, but I was consistent, and I loved running. At one track meet, the anchor for the 400-meter relay race was sick and unable to run. Our coach asked me to step in and run the anchor. No problem, I thought. When the baton was passed to me during the race, I took off. I was far ahead of the other runners until we came to the last turn prior to the straightaway and finish line. Suddenly I felt as if I had hit an invisible, energy-depleting force field. I had nothing left in the tank. I tried jogging, but even that was too much energy, so I ended up walking the last few feet of the race to the finish line.

I often tell that story as a part of my preaching. I use the story to talk about the importance of finishing the race, hanging in despite difficult situations and difficult times, or the importance of doing the hard thing. The story worked; however, it was flawed. It assumed that I should have been running the 400-meter race. The story failed to mention that, while I was filling in for someone else, I had not trained for the event. While I had done quite well in the races I was meant to run during that same track meet that day, I was simply not prepared for or conditioned to run this foreign race, which was forced upon me.

So, what should we do when we find ourselves running a race not meant for us? I use the acronym ACT: Acknowledge the injustice, Customize the circumstances to your benefit, and Take it easy on yourself. Let's break that down into a three-step process.

Acknowledging the injustice or the traumatic trigger takes away its power. When we pretend as though nothing is wrong or, worse, take on pressure, titles, responsibilities, or expectations that do not belong to us, we give the "other" our power. The "other" is then in control of the circumstance; the "other" is dictating terms and rules. For example, suppose you have been approved to take a half-day off at work. If a coworker informs you that your boss needs you to edit and return a 10-page document by 3 pm that day, and you do not acknowledge the injustice or wrong, what happens? Who has the power?

When a system denies you the same rights and privileges as someone else because of your race, ethnicity, sexuality, gender, or economic situation, and you do not challenge that situation, who has the power? Acknowledging and naming the injustice is important because it redistributes the power dynamic of the trauma. I was never meant to run the 400-meter relay, and you were never meant to be forced into painful, harmful, traumatic life experiences. They are not yours to carry.

This book, *The Four Promises*, helps us clearly see the importance of acknowledgment as we navigate the first promise—Permission. When we begin to acknowledge the injustices and traumatic triggers facing us, we also illuminate our own role in them. We give ourselves permission to hold our emotional and mental well-being up to the same standard as that of the "other." We give ourselves permission to have voice and power in our own traumatic situation. This is the power of acknowledgment and the need for that first principle of permission. So, to do this work of surviving present traumatic stress, we must first acknowledge that the trauma exists and that the trauma is wrong.

After acknowledgment, the next key to activating the four promises is customizing. We must customize the circumstances to the best of our ability. Here is the truth: We can become so enmeshed in our trauma that we lose dimension and perspective. Imagine standing at the entrance to a street and looking at a house at the other end of the street. The house looks very small in proportion to the other houses. Now imagine standing at the front door of that same house. The house now looks gigantic by comparison. Its proportions are harder to discern, and it may seem overwhelming. What's happening here? The house never changed size, but your distance from the house did, which altered your view of dimension and perspective. The closer you got to the house, the more enmeshed you became, incapable of determining proportions or having a healthy perspective. Trauma works the same way. The closer we are to the traumatic event, the more enmeshed we are in the circumstances, and the harder it is for us to have a healthy, balanced perspective.

There are parts of your ongoing trauma, your present traumatic stress, that you cannot change. Without knowing it, we may become so tangled up in our trauma that all we can see are the parts that are unchangeable. The reality is, in many cases we do have authority over aspects of our trauma. There are pieces we can customize to our benefit. Using the second and third promises, Rituals and Circles, helps us create enough space for ourselves in our trauma to begin to see places we can curate for our benefit.

The last key to activating the four promises is to take it easy on yourself. This work is difficult, and it takes time, space, and vulnerability for it to work. You are here. Look around you or watch the news for a couple of seconds, and you will realize how blessed you are. God has positioned you in favor.

You are seated in the hand of God, and though the enemy may rise at your gate, though pestilence lurks around you, you are safe in the hands of the Lord. You are here, fully present in this moment in time, and God has sustained you in this place for a purpose and a reason. So, take it easy on yourself. Despite it all, you are still here.

That is a place to celebrate and acknowledge. The last promise of the book helps us take authority over our narrative. The last promise causes us to reflect on how we tell our story. The last promise gives us authority to own our narrative. You are here.

Fourteen-Day Spiritual Guide

The Four Promises:

A Journey of Healing Past and Present Trauma

Day 1

Scripture

2 Samuel 12:16–17

David therefore pleaded with God for the child, and David fasted and went in and lay all night on the ground. So the elders of his house arose and went to him, to raise him up from the ground. But he would not, nor did he eat food with them.

Thought for the Day

David gave himself permission to grieve. He wasn't grieving as the king; he was grieving as a father for his son. When was the last time I allowed myself to grieve without attempting to host or cater to others' reaction to my grief?

Prayer

Mighty God, help me to find space to be weak today so that I may fully embrace your strength. Amen.

Day 2

Scripture

Genesis 21:16–17

Then she went and sat down across from him at a distance of about a bowshot; for she said to herself, "Let me not see the death of the boy." So she sat opposite him, and lifted her voice and wept. And God heard the voice of the lad. Then the angel of God called to Hagar out of heaven, and said to her, "What ails you, Hagar? Fear not, for God has heard the voice of the lad where he is."

Thought for the Day

Because Hagar was willing to express her emotions, God heard both her and her son's sorrow. Have I been honest with God about how I am really feeling? Like Hagar, have I been able to sit down and just say it out loud?

Prayer

Today, God, I pray that you will hold my sorrow and my anxiety with your hands of grace and compassion. Amen.

Day 3

Scripture

Exodus 34:1–2

And the Lord said to Moses, "Cut two tablets of stone like the first ones, and I will write on these tablets the words that were on the first tablets which you broke. So be ready in the morning, and come up in the morning to Mount Sinai, and present yourself to Me there on the top of the mountain."

Thought for the Day

Moses broke the first set of 10 commandment tablets out of anger, and yet God did not abandon him or restrict him from leading. What would happen today if I stopped worrying about others' reactions to my emotions and instead leaned in to express exactly how I am feeling?

Prayer

God, I may break some tablets today. Thank you for loving me anyway. Amen.

Day 4

Scripture

1 Kings 19:3–5

Elijah was afraid and ran for his life. When he came to Beersheba in Judah, he left his servant there, while he himself went a day's journey into the wilderness. He came to a broom bush, sat down under it and prayed that he might die. "I have had enough, Lord," he said. "Take my life; I am no better than my ancestors." Then he lay down under the bush and fell asleep. All at once an angel touched him and said, "Get up and eat." (NIV)

Thought for the Day

Fear does not disqualify me. It did not disqualify Elijah; instead, God cared for him because he was honest about how he was feeling.

Prayer

Thank you, Lord, for loving all of me, even my imperfections, worries, fears, sorrows, and anxieties. You love me just the same. Thank you. Amen.

Day 5

Scripture

Judges 4:6–8

Then she sent and called for Barak the son of Abinoam from Kedesh in Naphtali, and said to him, "Has not the Lord God of Israel commanded, 'Go and deploy troops at Mount Tabor; take with you ten thousand men of the sons of Naphtali and of the sons of Zebulun; and against you I will deploy Sisera, the commander of Jabin's army, with his chariots and his multitude at the River Kishon; and I will deliver him into your hand'?" And Barak said to her, "If you will go with me, then I will go; but if you will not go with me, I will not go!"

Thought for the Day

Barak asked for what he needed despite how it made him look or what it would cost him. Today I want to be bold enough to ask for what I need, instead of pretending I can handle it all by myself.

Prayer

Thank you, Lord, for providing help and helpers; give me the courage today, mighty God, to ask for what I need. Amen.

Day 6

Scripture

Genesis 21:5–6

Now Abraham was one hundred years old when his son Isaac was born to him. And Sarah said, "God has made me laugh, and all who hear will laugh with me."

Thought for the Day

Sarah gave herself permission to laugh, permission to be made the object of a joke. What would happen if I did not take myself so seriously today and had a little fun?

Prayer

O, God, today bless me with endless opportunities to laugh and celebrate the simplicity and joy of your creation. Amen.

Day 7

Scripture

Psalm 34:17–19

The righteous cry out, and the Lord hears,
And delivers them out of all their troubles.
The Lord is near to those who have a broken heart,
And saves such as have a contrite spirit.

Many are the afflictions of the righteous,
But the Lord delivers him out of them all.

Thought for the Day

You said in your word, God, that you are near to the brokenhearted. My heart at times is broken; today I want to feel your nearness.

Prayer

Thank you, loving God, for your presence in the midst of despair. Amen.

Day 8

Scripture

2 Samuel 6:14

Then David danced before the Lord with all his might; and David was wearing a linen ephod.

Thought for the Day

David was so excited to have the Ark of the Covenant back that he danced out of his clothes. When is the last time I danced without thinking about the opinions of those around me?

Prayer

Today, Lord, help me to find space and time to dance, shout, scream, cry, or just sit with you and you alone. Thank you, Lord. Amen.

Day 9

Scripture

Luke 2:37–38

…and this woman was a widow of about eighty-four years, who did not depart from the temple, but served God with fasting and prayers night and day. And coming in that instant she gave thanks to the Lord, and spoke of Him to all those who looked for redemption in Jerusalem.

Thought for the Day

Anna had a ritual that served her. Her practice of fasting and praying daily helped her deal with her loneliness and grief over the death of her husband. What practice will I put in place today that will help me to make it through this day?

Prayer

Loving God, thank you for providing in this day everything I need to experience your peace; help me, Lord, to focus and see your provisions.

Day 10

Scripture

Luke 5:3–4

Then He got into one of the boats, which was Simon's, and asked him to put out a little from the land. And He sat down and taught the multitudes from the boat. When He had stopped speaking, He said to Simon, "Launch out into the deep and let down your nets for a catch."

Thought for the Day

Simon was a fisherman; the boat was part of his daily equipment. Yet Jesus was asking him to use what he knew in a different way. Jesus was stretching him. Are there practices that I've taken for granted in which God may be wanting to stretch me?

Prayer

God, I don't want to rely on empty rituals; they are not helping me. Stretch me today, Lord, so that I may see you in a new way I have never seen before.

Day 11

Scripture

John 11:33–36

Therefore, when Jesus saw her weeping, and the Jews who came with her weeping, He groaned in the spirit and was troubled. And He said, "Where have you laid him?"

They said to Him, "Lord, come and see."

Jesus wept. Then the Jews said, "See how He loved him!"

Thought for the Day

Jesus wept with those who were weeping. He was not alone in his sorrow. He was in a community, a circle of people where he could weep freely. In what circles can I freely weep, freely be vulnerable, and freely heal?

Prayer

God, help me to carve out a new circle for healing. Give me fresh discernment about those in my circle already, Lord. I want to be whole. Thank you, God. Amen.

Day 12

Scripture

Matthew 26:7–10

… a woman came to Him having an alabaster flask of very costly fragrant oil, and she poured it on His head as He sat at the table. But when His disciples saw it, they were indignant, saying, "Why this waste? For this fragrant oil might have been sold for much and given to the poor."

But when Jesus was aware of it, He said to them, "Why do you trouble the woman? For she has done a good work for Me."

Thought for the Day

This woman was willing to risk her status, her identity, and even her wealth to anoint Jesus. Her focus and concern were on Him. Who in my circle is that dedicated to my healing? Is it time to find new circles?

Prayer

God, send the ones I need into my life. Guide me to places of safety and healing so that I might be all that you have designed me to be. Amen.

Day 13

Scripture

Job 2:11–13

Now when Job's three friends heard of all this adversity that had come upon him, each one came from his own place – Eliphaz the Temanite, Bildad the Shuhite, and Zophar the Naamathite. For they had made an appointment together to come and mourn with him, and to comfort him. And when they raised their eyes from afar, and did not recognize him, they lifted their voices and wept; and each one tore his robe and sprinkled dust on his head toward heaven. So they sat down with him on the ground seven days and seven nights, and no one spoke a word to him, for they saw that his grief was very great.

Thought for the Day

During those first seven days, Job's friends demonstrated the value of a circle. They provided Job with a space to grieve and joined him in his sorrow. That is empathy. Where are the spaces in my life that I can receive that kind of empathy? Who are the people who would sit in silence with me?

Prayer

Loving God, open my eyes today to the beauty of your creation and all the many ways in which you surround me with your love. Amen.

ᵧ 14

Scripture

Mark 14:37–40

Then He came and found them sleeping and said to Peter, "Simon, are you sleeping? Could you not watch one hour? Watch and pray, lest you enter into temptation. The spirit indeed is willing, but the flesh is weak." Again He went away and prayed and spoke the same words. And when He returned, He found them asleep again, for their eyes were heavy; and they did not know what to answer Him.

Thought for the Day

Trauma, grief, and even worry are all heavy. Jesus's disciples could do no better than to sleep during his greatest moment of trauma, prior to the cross. This is a reminder that we are all human and in need of grace; that includes me.

Prayer

God, help me to remember today that all of us are flawed and in need of you. Amen.

About the Author

Ron Bell is both a pastor and an author. He is the senior pastor of Camphor Memorial UMC and a regular guest columnist for the *Saint Paul Monitor*. He has written articles for *The Upper Room* and has published articles in the *Minnesota Coalition for Death Education and Support* quarterly journal. On his blog site www.DrRonBell.com, you can find many of his most popular articles on race, trauma, empathy, and grief as well as information on his other book, *Is There Space for Me? Embracing Grief Through Art.* He has also created an ongoing webinar series on Trauma and Empathy that he has led with several universities including St. Paul College, Bethel University, University of Maryland Eastern Shore, Fuller Theological Seminary, and several others, as well as with numerous nonprofits and county agencies. Ron is married to Dr. Eboni M. Bell, and they have two sons.

Ron has a bachelor's degree in Philosophy from Morgan State University, a master's degree in Theology from Regent University School of Divinity, a doctorate degree in Ministry from Lancaster Theological Seminary, and has done his certification work for trauma response at Rutgers University School of Social Work. Ron is an ordained Elder in the United Methodist Church and a proud member of Alpha Phi Alpha Fraternity, Inc.

References

All Scripture references retrieved from https://www.biblegateway.com

Brown, Brené. "Listening to shame." Ted Talk (March 2012). Retrieved from https://www.ted.com/talks/brene_brown_listening_to_shame?language=en

Celeghin, A., Diano, M., Bagnis, A., Viola, M., & Tamietto, M. (2017). Basic emotions in human neuroscience: Neuroimaging and beyond. *Frontiers in Psychology, 8*, 1432.

Chiboola, H. (2020). Theoretical perspective of traditional counseling. In S. G. Taukeni (Ed.), *Counseling and therapy.* Retrieved from https://www.intechopen.com/books/counseling-and-therapy/theoretical-perspective-of-traditional-counseling.

Ekman, P. (1992). Are there basic emotions? *Psychol. Rev. 99,* 550–553. doi: 10.1037/0033-295X.99.3.550

Fehr, B., & Russell, J. A. (1984). Concept of emotion viewed from a prototype perspective. *Journal of Experimental Psychology: General, 113*(3), 464–486.

Hart, S. (2019). *Brain, attachment, personality: An introduction to neuroaffective development.* London: Routledge.

Harvey, M. (1996). "An ecological view of psychological trauma and trauma recovery. *Journal of Traumatic Stress 9*(1). 3–23.

MacLean, P. D. (1990). *The triune brain in evolution: Role in paleocerebral functions.* New York: Plenum Press.

Menakem, R. (2017). *My grandmother's hands.* Las Vegas: Central Recovery Press.

Shaw, B. (2019). When trauma gets stuck in the body. *Psychology Today.* Retrieved from https://www.psychologytoday.com/us/blog/in-the-body/201910/when-trauma-gets-stuck-in-the-body.

Tangney, J. P., Niedenthal, P. M., Covert, M. V., & Barlow, D. H. (1998). Are shame and guilt related to distinct self-discrepancies? A test of Higgins's (1987) hypotheses. *Journal of Personality and Social Psychology, 75*(1), 256–268.

Van der Kolk, Bessel (2014). *The body keeps the score: Brain, mind, and body in the healing of trauma.* New York: Viking.